FRENCH PAINTING:

THE TWENTIETH CENTURY

CONTENTS

Published by
CASTLE BOOKS
A Division of
BOOK SALES, INC.
110 Enterprise Avenue
Secaucus, New Jersey 07094

INTRODUCTION

The artistic climate of Paris during the first half of this century was one of rare inventiveness, exploration and discovery, as artists formulated not only a new philosophy of seeing their world, but a new vocabulary of forms and new techniques of expression.

The artists whose work appears here are products of the first half of the century. Although several lived well into the nineteen-fifties, sixties and even seventies, the artistic world since the Second World War has had its major centers elsewhere; during the first half of the century, Paris acted as a clearing house for most of what was new in the painterly arts.

The revolutionary ideas of twentieth-century art took three major paths, their common denominator the concern of the artist with the workings of his mind and the relationship of the individual with the outside world.

The first of these paths, Expressionism, was concerned with the artist's emotional responses, through which he strove to illustrate a subjective, personalized feeling about a given object, scene or circumstance. The second, Cubism, explored the internal structuring of objects, breaking down form in an attempt to achieve a formalized inner harmony, an exploration reminiscent of Platonic philosophy. The third, Surrealism, was concerned with an exploration of the subconscious mind both with a formalized dream imagery and with the automatic, or spontaneous, outpouring of energy through the artistic process. This attempt of the artist to explore inner reality was perhaps the diametric opposite of Cubism's concern with formalizing outer reality.

Much of the artistic ferment that occurred in Paris during these first decades of the century can be traced back directly to the work of the Post-Impressionist painters, and most importantly to that of Gauguin and Cezanne. In the last decade of the nineteenth century, a young group of painters revolving around the philosopher artist and teacher Paul Serusier, adapted for themselves the name Nabis, or seers, basing their artistic theories on symbolic and mystical ideas and espousing the color and flat surface areas of Gauguin's painting. Among them was Pierre Bonnard, the great colorist, who, basing his own work on the color theories of Paul Gauguin and on the Japanese prints then fashionable in France, painted until the mid-twentieth century producing canvases of brilliance and beauty.

Expressionism was first revealed as a significant artistic movement in 1903, in an exhibition of the works of such young artists as Matisse, Derain and Vlaminck. In the exhibition gallery there was a statue by the Renaissance sculptor, Donatello, and from the offhand remark of one critic that he was seeing Donatello among the wild beasts (fauves) came the name of the group: the Fauves.

The Fauvist movement, however, was far from wild or uncontrolled. Indeed much the opposite was true in the carefully planned surface patterns that marked the work of Matisse. However, in the vivid use of undiluted colors and the relative lack of concern with representational accuracy, the term seemed justly applied at the time. The Fauvist movement was echoed in Germany, where the painting of the German Expressionists pushed further into the realms of pure expressionism.

The uncontested master of the Fauves, Henri Matisse, soon left the movement behind him in his explorations of texture, pattern and color. He became one of the giants of twentieth-century painting, and the polar opposite of another giant, Pablo Picasso, founder of the Cubist movement and a master of form and structure.

In 1907, just four years after the first Fauvist exhibition, Picasso exhibited his *Demoiselles d'Avignon,* called the landmark painting of Cubism, a rather ugly canvas which distorted and fractured five female nudes in ways that had never been conceived of before. Picasso worked very closely with Georges Braque, the two young artists basing their work on the theories of the Post-Impressionist master, Paul Cezanne, who maintained that all form could be broken down into the basic shapes of a cube, cone and cylinder. Cubism, as the work of Braque and Picasso came to be called, first emerged as a mature form as "Analytical Cubism," in which the surface of the canvas acted as a prism through which all objects were fractured into multiple facets. Various aspects of an object, whether animate or inanimate, were shown simultaneously, as if one had walked around, under and above, and had chosed to portray all of these views as intersecting and overlapping. In a direct antithesis to the work of Matisse and the Fauves, the Cubists used monochromatic tones of gray and beige.

The second phase of Cubism, "Synthetic Cubism," was a style also developed through the close collaboration of Braque and Picasso. In this form, the surface of the canvas was considered two-dimensional and decorative. Collage was introduced and the canvas became a sort of tray on which objects and textures were pasted; later painting came to represent the actual collage objects. Synthetic Cubism was a looser, more open style, allowing for wider range of color and further experimentation with form.

Cubism attracted other artists who adapted it to suit their own styles and theories. Among these were the Orphists, led by Robert Delaunay, who were concerned with color as a means of expression, Fernand Leger, who was concerned with the effects of industrialization, and the Dutchman, Piet Mondrian, who simplified Cubism to a formalized system of color and structure in a mathematical harmony of proportion.

Braque and Picasso themselves adapted and modified their styles throughout their long careers: Braque remaining closer to the original concepts of Cubism; Picasso ranging far and wide through a variety of modes, finally synthesizing his work into a blending of Cubism, Classicism and Surrealism, his interests varying from pure exploration of line, form and color to the most poignant of political and social commentary.

The third movement, Surrealism, arose out of the bitterness and disillusionment that followed the First World War and was among the most prominent of artistic developments during the period between the two wars. Beginning with a Nihilistic anti-art experiment known as Dada, in which the happened-upon, odd object was elevated to the status of art by fanciful, imposed titles, Surrealism emerged full-grown with the publication in 1924 of Andre Breton's Surrealist Manifesto. In this document, Breton maintained that rational thought was no longer a significant concern; that the true realm of the writer and artist was the exploration of the unconscious mind and that the automatic, subliminal workings of the mind should be given full range of expression. The Surrealists worked in two distinctly different styles. Veristic Surrealism, exemplified by the work of Salvador Dali and Rene Magritte, used dream-images of startling realism in which objects out of context and placed in alien environments present a portrait of a nightmare reality in order to express the wounds of psychic injury. At the other pole, the Automatic Surrealists, encouraged by the new freedoms found in Cubism and abstract non-representational painting, were concerned with the action of "automatism" in which the artist let the images of the mind flow through his brush in a kind of pictorial script. This is clearly expressed in the work of such artists as Joan Miro and Andre Masson.

During the first three decades of the twentieth century, Paris was an artistic crossroads, as artists from all over Europe and even the United States came to live, study and exchange ideas. Many of these have already been mentioned: the

Spaniards—Picasso, Dali and Miro; the Dutchman, Mondrian; the Belgian, Magritte, and the German, Max Ernst. Nestled in the rabbit-warren of studios in Montmartre in the years before and just after the First World War, were a group of artists who had gathered from all over Europe to form what has come to be known as the School of Paris.

Among them was an enclave of Jewish painters, including the Russians, Marc Chagall and Chaim Soutine, and the Italian, Amedeo Modigliani. Chagall's art, based on memories of his childhood in a small Jewish community in a Russian village, is peopled by the folklore and the fantasies, rich in dream-symbolism, of his heritage. Modigliani created manneristic, elongated portraits, many of them of models who had shared his bed and humble lodgings the night before, portraits gentle but often filled with a quiet sense of despair. Chagall returned to Russia just before the outbreak of the Russian Revolution and returned to Paris in 1923, his reputation assured. Modigliani died of consumption in his garret studio in 1920.

Two French artists closely associated with the School of Paris developed their own unique styles. Georges Rouault, an Expressionist, used heavy black lines and vivid color to create a unique and religious vision of the suffering of mankind. Maurice Utrillo, the son of the painter and model Suzanne Valadon, fighting a lifelong battle with alcoholism, created his own reality of the streets of Montmartre and the Paris suburbs.

The movements of Cubism and Expressionism, with their conflicting ideas of formal structure versus emotionalism and a rich surface pattern, Surrealism, prominent during the 30's and into the 40's, and the work of the artists of the School of Paris kept the artistic climate of Paris very exciting indeed. The outbreak of World War II disrupted Europe's artistic community tremendously with the artists of Germany fleeing to Paris, Switzerland and the United States. After the war, the ideas developed during the first half of the century continued to be explored in Paris, and increasingly in the United States, culminating in the major artistic developments that would surface in New York in the 1950's and 1960's.

In the last quarter of the century, new artists with new ideas are enriching the heritage of those who came before. But it is artists such as Braque, Matisse, Chagall, Miro and Picasso, who started their careers in the opening years of the twentieth century and lived and worked well into the last half of the century, who will remain as the giants of their age; it will be a weighty accomplishment for younger generations of artists to achieve the respect accorded these Parisian painters of the twentieth century.

PIERRE BONNARD

Pierre Bonnard (1867-1947) was born in Fontenay-aux-Roses not far from Paris. He was a law student before transferring to the Beaux-Arts and he later attended the Académie Julian where he met Denis, Vuillard and Paul Serusier, the young philosopher-painter and mystic. Espousing the color theories of Paul Gauguin, these revolutionary young painters formed a group and called themselves the Nabis, or prophets, after some of the symbolic ideas of Serusier. Bonnard, who joined the group in 1891, was called the Japanese Nabi by his contemporaries because of his fascination with the Japanese prints, then becoming fashionable in France, that Serusier collected. Bonnard's earliest works were designs for theatrical sets, furniture decorations, screens and posters, for he shared a studio with the theatrical producer Lügne-Poe, as well as with Vuillard and Denis. He also contributed regularly to the periodical, *La Revue Blanche,* made a set of lithographs based on aspects of life in Paris for Ambroise Vollard, and did book illustrations. He had his first exhibition of paintings in 1896. Bonnard, like Edouard Vuillard, with whom he was closely linked, was an"intimist," a painter constantly delighted with ordinary and homey actions and objects, to which he brought a constant freshness. Bonnard was attracted by the color of the Impressionists, but did not subordinate form and reality to impressionistic color. He worked slowly, capturing on canvas his own rebellion against current styles of art and predetermined theories. Bonnard's palette is virtually a rainbow, with pearly flesh tones, and shadows that range from pinks, blues and golds to opaque grays or deep blues. His paintings transpose solids and transparencies, light and shade. They have an abstract structural quality that is both decorative and satisfying in its use of space, a style that foreshadows the works of Matisse. Bonnard was an artist who looked at the world around him with as much joy when an old man as when a youth, and whose vision remained extremely personal and honest.

A Corner of the Dining Room at Cannet (ca. 1932)
Bonnard's house in Le Cannet, a small village in the hills beyond Cannes, was a modest home, reflecting his simple tastes. In this painting, Bonnard has typically used warm, gentle coloration to transform the commonplace objects of his everyday life into a glowing and magical scene. Violets, magentas and tones of gold are deliberately repeated on mantelpiece, table and shawl. The carefully laid out composition is subordinate to the interchange of light and shadow, the surface texture and the harmony of color in this warm and delicate interior and still life.

GEORGES BRAQUE

Georges Braque (1882-1963), along with Pablo Picasso, formulated one of the most important artistic movements of the twentieth century—Cubism—which freed the artist from strict representation of form, established a new intellectualization of artistic thought, and led to all of the later developments in abstract art. Braque was influenced by the Impressionists and by his contemporaries, Matisse and Derain, whose Fauve movement he joined in 1905. But Braque by this time had also been strongly influenced by the architectonic paintings of Cezanne, and even in this early period, his work differed from that of the Fauves in its use of monochromatic colors, angles as well as curves, and a flatter more transparent pigment. Braque was introduced to Picasso in the autumn of 1907 by the young art dealer, Daniel-Henry Kahnweiler. At Picasso's studio, Braque saw the unfinished painting, *Les Demoiselles d'Avignon,* and became absorbed in Picasso's experiments with the analysis of form. Braque and Picasso had arrived at more or less identical points of view by different pathways; using muted colors, geometrical patterns, inverted perspective and overlapping volumes, they developed the style known as Cubism. During this period the two artists worked closely together, producing works so similar as to be distinguishable only by fine points. Their close association was broken when Braque was called up to service in World War I. When he returned to painting, he remained faithful to the Cubist iconography of still-life objects and the single seated or standing figure, but he began to develop a new and more personal style, using a brighter palette and freer manner. Collage entered his work as an effective tool for experimenting with texture. By the 1920's Braque was the master of a personal Cubist idiom. By 1925, he had created a memorable series of still lifes, which had brought him international success. As Braque continued innovating and experimenting, he found a balance between intelligence and sensitivity, technique and inspiration. The resulting paintings combine the multiple planes and inverted space of Cubism with delicate colors, rounded forms and sinuous line, and are characterized by a serene stillness.

Still Life with Purple Plums (1935)
This composition is typical of the complex structure with which Braque invested his work in the 1920's and 1930's. It is rich and decorative, and the forms have departed from the tight formalistic compositions of Analytical Cubism. This canvas offers strong vertical and horizontal movement and a wealth of interlocking and overlapping curves, expanding and contracting patterns. The varied elements combine to form a unity of line, form and subtle color that goes beyond a simple description of objects and explores the interrelationships of shapes and colors.

MARC CHAGALL

Marc Chagall (1889-   ) was born in Vitebsk, Russia, a tiny village that is presented often in his paintings. Although he came from a large and relatively poor family, his parents recognized his talent and saw that he received art lessons, first in Vitebsk and later in St. Petersburg, where he had his first contact with European and French contemporary art. This experience encouraged him to go to Paris in 1910. He was soon a member of the large group of foreign artists living in Montmartre who came to be known as the School of Paris, and his circle of friends included Modigliani, Soutine, and Delaunay among others. Almost immediately, Chagall began to paint in his own personal style, using a bright palette and taking his subject matter from childhood memories and Russian and Jewish folklore. These fanciful themes were at first presented in large Cubist planes, a style which soon vanished from his compositions. Chagall's first big exhibition was held in Berlin in 1914, and his use of color and fantasy influenced post-war German artists considerably. Chagall himself spent the war years in Russia and was appointed Commissar of Fine Arts for the Vitebsk area after the Russian Revolution of 1917. He then went to Moscow to paint murals for the Jewish Theatre, finally returning to France in 1922. His reputation was firmly established by that time, and he received commissions to illustrate several books, the most important of these being an illustrated Bible for which he traveled to the Holy Land. Chagall spent the years of the Nazi occupation in the United States and returned to France to settle in 1947. He now divides his time between Vence and Paris, painting, designing stained-glass windows, and giving away his great public works, such as the windows and murals for the United Nations, the Jersualem Synagogue and the Paris and New York opera houses. Chagall's painting, with its delicate, undulating line and its brilliant, varied palette, offers a dream world in which the laws of logic and gravity are overturned and fairy tales appear to be real, a happy mixture of dream and reality, fantasy and nostalgia.

Feathers in Bloom (1943)
In this imaginative fantasy, Chagall has created two creatures who might have stepped from the pages of a fairy tale: a sloe-eyed hen with delicate flower-like plumage and a blue horse who prances on human legs. They gaze at each other with rapt expressions of love and tenderness that are almost human. The moon that floats in the lower right hand corner adds a celestial quality to this fantastic pair of lovers.

RAOUL DUFY

Raoul Dufy (1877-1953), a leading member of the Fauves, was born in Le Havre, where he began to study art at night while working as an errand boy during the day. When he obtained a small scholarship in 1900, he went to Paris to study with Bonnat, and about five years later he met Matisse and the other Fauve painters, whose colors delighted him. Dufy experimented with Fauvism, made some attempts at Cubism, and in the years between 1905 and about 1920, earned his living by working on a museum staff, designing fabrics and doing some book illustration. Painting at Honfleur toward the end of World War I, Dufy observed that line moves more rapidly than does color and that the human eye receives the sensation of color more easily than that of movement, thus holding this mental image longer. These perceptions led to his development of that short, lightning-fast, calligraphic line that was to mark all of his work. It also led to his application of color in "diffusions" that were not strictly confined to outlines but sometimes swept across a work in broad bands coloring objects perhaps half-green and half-blue, making them part of a lively world in which both color and line sparkle. Dufy's personal symbolism, sensitive touch and feeling for color created a world of fashionable pleasure on canvas, from which he made a natural transition to textile design, ceramic decoration and decorative painting. By 1925, his reputation solidly established, Dufy was commissioned to paint murals for many French public buildings. He began to suffer from multiple arthritis in 1937, and moved to southwestern France for his health. When the disease progressed to the point that he could no longer paint, he came to the United States for cortisone treatment in 1947. After the treatment and a trip to Arizona, Dufy, although not cured, was well enough to return to France and to continue painting until his death in 1953. Of the group of painters known as the Fauves, Dufy, with his love of color and his calligraphic, dancing line, was among the most lighthearted. The need to delight the eye, as an end in itself, was a major consideration in his art.

The Jetty at Honfleur (1930)
Honfleur is a small port in Normandy, a favorite French summer resort today, but in the sixteenth and seventeenth centuries an important port for ships coming up the Seine. This painting is a good example of Dufy's calligraphic use of line and delight in vivid color. The jetty curves in a gentle arabesque toward the horizon, highlighted by the economically drawn lighthouse. In the foreground, the summer visitors seated on benches and watching or strolling along the jetty provide splashes of red, white, black and gold against the blues, violets and pinks of the twilight sea and sky.

FERNAND LEGER

Fernand Leger (1881-1955) was born of peasant stock in Argentan, Normandy, but left the land at sixteen to become an architect's apprentice in Caen. Three years later he took a similar post in Paris and then, after completing his military service, abandoned architecture for painting and studied briefly at the Beaux-Arts. Between 1905 and 1910, he met Henri Rousseau, discovered the work of Cezanne, and became associated with the sculptors Lipchitz and Laurens and the artists Delaunay, Chagall, and Soutine. In 1910, he met Braque and Picasso, and in 1911 he participated in the first Cubist exhibition as a purely Cubist painter. He did not develop his own mechanistic and highly personal style until 1917. His first works were primarily of objects and machinery with human figures serving merely as incidental additions to an industrial civilization. By 1921, however, the human figure, larger than life-size and majestically ordinary, became an important part of these scenes. Between 1924 and 1926, he returned to the painting of still lifes, and also began to paint large, rigorously abstract and decorative murals. He then painted several series of works including *Objects in Space* in which architectural elements are replaced by scattered objects, *Contrasting Rhythms, Swimmers, Bicycles,* and *American Works,* all of them concerned with modern life and its violent contrasts, its great machines and buildings, and its most common and therefore most often forgotten aspects. Leger believed that the painter should not try to paint beautiful objects, but rather that he should create beautiful pictures in which the human figure has no more importance than the bicycle wheel. He presented observations of daily life through stylistic lines and large planes of color that create both rhythm and space, creating a distinct form of modern art that is both timeless and universal in its force and dignity.

Leisure: Homage to Louis David (1948-49)
The theme of this painting, cyclists, originated during Leger's visit to the United States during the war years 1940-45. Its reference to the Classical artist David was intended by Leger to stress his definite return to simple and comprehensible subject matter. This work marks a return from the abstract paintings of the 1940's to the more static composition of his figurative works of the 1930's. The colors—bright blue, yellow, gray, green, and red—contained within the clear line, create animated space and a balance that is accentuated by the compositional arrangement of the human figures. In this arrangement, unexpected birds, flowers, and plants add humanity and create a lightness of mood suitable to the obviously jovial atmosphere such a family outing must have. Modern man here is in harmony both with nature and with the mechanical world.

16

HENRI MATISSE

Henri Matisse (1869-1954), who created a style based on the decorative use of color and surface pattern, was born in Le Cateau in the north of France. At the age of twenty-two he decided to study art and moved to Paris to study with Bougereau at the Beaux-Arts. Matisse found the conservative ideas of this academician stultifying, however, and left to enter the studio of Gustave Moreau, the symbolist painter, who was a gifted teacher and open to his student's experimentation. Matisse studied various painting styles at the Louvre, was influenced by Gauguin and especially by the structural works of Cezanne, whose painting was to have an even more pronounced effect on the young Pablo Picasso, twelve years Matisse's junior. Matisse began painting in an Impressionistic style but by 1905, at the exhibition of the *Salon d'Automne*, he was the most impressive of the young artists whose bold experiments in color were to earn them the name Fauves, or wild beasts. The Fauves were more a chance encounter than a unified group, however, and the members of the 1905 exhibition soon began to go their separate ways. By 1908, Matisse had begun the exploration of painting as a decorative and sensuous art, emphasizing the use of flat bold areas of color as a structural element. By this time, Matisse and Picasso were leading members of the artistic circle of Paris that centered about the home of the American, Gertrude Stein, an avid patron of both young artists. By 1911, after a trip to Morocco, oriental motifs and rich surface patterns entered Matisse's works. As his style developed, the human figure became merely a part of an overall still life, as Matisse juxtaposed intense color, varied patterns and a rhythmic use of line. Throughout his long career, Matisse sought to improve his work and find increasingly varied means of expression and, working in his studio in Nice, accepted commissions to do book illustrations, ballet sets and murals, as well as paintings and line drawings.

Interior, Flowers and Parrot (1924)
Matisse's concern with pattern and surface texture is evident here. Although perspective is achieved through the angle of the table and through the drawn curtain framing the interior scene and leading to the distant window, it is less important to Matisse than the patterns of the crosshatchings on the floor and the repeated paisley and floral designs on screen, wallpaper and wall hangings. The drawn curtain with interior beyond serves as a counterbalance in design, repeating the motifs of the foreground and balancing the intricate still life. The repeated reds are heightened by touches of blue and gold, but the tones are both warm and peaceful, echoing the calm of midday in a hot climate.

JOAN MIRO

Joan Miro (1893-   ) was born in Montroig in the Province of Catalonia, Spain. He began to study art at the Barcelona School of Fine Arts when he was fourteen, but after a short time, enrolled at the Gali Academy in the same city. When he was eighteen, he decided that academic instruction was not giving him anything very useful, and began to work alone. Miro made his first visit to Paris in 1919, immediately joining the leading circle of artists through the introductions of Picasso, a fellow Spaniard. For a time, influenced by Braque and Picasso, Miro painted in the Cubist manner. By 1924, however, he had become a leading member of the Surrealists and worked with Max Ernst on the sets and costumes of *Romeo and Juliet,* a Diaghilev Ballet Russe production. Miro remained in Paris, continuing to paint with the Surrealists for sixteen years, leaving France in 1940 for the island of Mallorca, where he experimented in lithography and ceramics. Miro returned to Paris in 1944, continuing to paint but also designing tapestries and rugs, making ceramics and creating sculpture in stone and wood. Among his many architectural commissions were the ceramic murals for the UNESCO building in Paris. Miro now lives on the island of Mallorca in his long-desired "big studio," designed for him by the architect Jose Luis Sert. Miro's art is considered the best example of that form of Surrealistic painting known as Automatic or Absolute Surrealism in which the unconscious image emerges directly, through the medium of the artist, onto the canvas or paper. His work successfully represents the effort to discard inherited traditions and regain the innocence and spontaneity of the creative act, one of the cherished ideals of the Surrealist artist. Perhaps more than any other in the field of modern art, his work embodies a sense of innocence and joyous freedom. Miro's paintings are composed of amorphous shapes that swim in a primordial soup from which he shapes his humorous and often life-like figures—hieroglyphs of people, animals and other forms that are as mobile and fluid as the changing shapes of the amoeba, part of a timeless universe portrayed in brilliant color.

Woman, Bird and Star (1942)
In this painting, Miro has used some of his most basic ideograms to portray a celestial scene, incorporating the stars, the night and the secret beings which dwell between the stars and the night—part of his mythology of nature. His watery use of color in this work provides his creatures with a floating suspended medium in which to live. The use of dense black in the lower portion and as a part of the lower figure adds a note of gravity. In its pictorial shorthand and use of swollen biomorphic forms, the work is a prime example of Miro's unique Surrealistic world.

AMEDEO MODIGLIANI

Amedeo Modigliani (1884-1920) was born in Italy in the Livorno ghetto. His father, a ruined banker, died young, and his mother, a descendant of the Dutch philosopher Spinoza, encouraged her delicate son in his aptitude for art, sending him to study in Florence and Venice and to visit museums throughout Italy. When Modigliani arrived in Paris in 1907, he had a small inheritance from a rich uncle, but he was already seriously ill with tuberculosis. Handsome, talented, sensitive, and extremely proud of his Jewish heritage, Modigliani became one of the most notorious characters in Montmartre and was soon penniless and often homeless. He frequently slept and worked in the studios of artist friends who liked him and recognized his great talent as both a painter and a sculptor. He moved to Montparnasse in 1913 and kept body and soul together by selling drawings in cafes for infinitesimal sums. Finally, in 1917, he married Jeanne Hebuterne and the couple set up housekeeping in a miserable garret. It was too late for this more normal life to conquer the ravages of consumption. Modigliani died in a Paris hospital on a January day in 1920. His desperate widow threw herself from the roof of her parents' apartment house on the day of his funeral, leaving their daughter to be reared by her maternal grandparents. Two years later Modigliani's work was discovered by Dr. Albert C. Barnes, the great art collector of Pennsylvania. Considered the leader of the School of Paris, Modigliani's subjective and expressive art reveals his basic dignity, his despair, and a feeling of haunting melancholy. The bulk of his surviving works, dating from 1915 to 1920, indicate his interest in African sculpture, the Cubist works of Braque and Picasso, and the simplification of form that he learned from the sculptor, Brancusi. The influences of Botticelli and Italian Mannerism also appear in his paintings. These combined in his elegant, sinuous style to produce easily recognizable portraits and nudes with long slender oval heads, sloping shoulders, and extremely subtle coloration. Within the framework of this mannered stylization, Modigliani portrayed a great variety of distinct personalities.

Bride and Groom (1915)
This double portrait is illustrative of Modigliani's elongated manneristic figures, but is atypical in the artist's use of Cubist-like planes which lend a stiffness to the figures, echoed by the vacant eyes and rather smug expressions. The monochromatic palette—tones of black, gray and beige and flesh colors alleviated only by a bold stripe—is also suggestive of a Cubist influence. Modigliani has replaced the sensuous qualities of many of his portraits with a sense of the propriety and smug self-satisfaction of his subjects.

PABLO PICASSO

The name of Pablo Picasso (1881-1973) has become almost synonymous with the development of modern art, and certainly Cubism owes its development directly to Picasso's genius. Picasso arrived in Paris from Madrid at the age of 19, settling in a Montmartre tenement. In his ramshackle studio a circle of artists gathered, and their meetings fomented artistic movements that were to have startling and far-reaching effects. Picasso was concerned with studying Cezanne's concept of volume and space as abstract geometry, and had also enthusiastically discovered African sculpture, which reduced pictorial representation to its basics. Picasso, working with these ideas, and aided by the logical, orderly mind of Georges Braque, began to experiment with a particular style that was later to be given the name "Cubism." In 1907 Picasso completed the work that has come to be known as the landmark canvas of the Cubist movement—the unlovely and radical *Les Demoiselles d'Avignon*—five female figures, whose forms are ruptured and dislocated, in styles ranging from the formality of Egyptian sculpture to the grotesqueness of African masks. In the succeeding years, Picasso and Braque experimented with "Analytic Cubism" in which familiar objects such as glasses and pitchers were broken down into geometric planes, and later with "Synthetic Cubism," a collage method in which bits of cloth or paper were used to build up an image. From 1915 until 1936, Picasso painted in various Cubist manners, often employing swollen metamorphic shapes that were emotional in content. The mural, *Guernica,* is an example of this style. In these works, Picasso employs human anatomy as the raw material for his fertile, imagination. Original function no longer matters as Picasso transforms eyes and breasts, profiles and frontal views, light and shadow. This metamorphic style was to form the basis of his art throughout the remainder of his long career, although he experimented with Surrealism and with large, almost sculptural portraits, produced lithographs, etchings, sculpture, jewelry and ceramics. Picasso continued to work in all mediums in his studio in the south of France until his death at the age of 92. His influence upon modern art has been immeasurable.

Still Life with Lemon and Oranges (1936)
This canvas is typical of the many still lifes done during Picasso's post-Cubist period. The palette is brighter, the angular planes of Cubism have been softened and roundness of form is predominant. But many of the basic tenets of Cubism are present here: the simultaneous viewing of several aspects of an object and a perspective that allows the table to appear slanted both upward and downward at the same time. This canvas indicates Picasso's renewed interest in natural forms and is also indicative of an evolving style in which the strictly geometric cubistic shapes assume fluid metamorphic qualities.

GEORGES ROUAULT

Georges Rouault (1871-1958) was born in Paris, the son of a cabinetmaker. He was sent to an austere Protestant school but left to be apprenticed to a restorer of medieval stained-glass windows. Rouault was apprenticed to the restorer in 1885, and went to the School of Decorative Arts at night until 1891, when he became a pupil of Gustave Moreau. Moreau's use of decorative color and the ironwork of the windows were to influence Rouault's style throughout his career, whether he worked in pastels, watercolors, oils or graphic mediums. Using contrasts of rich color and heavy black line, illusion and reality, he expressed a compassion for mankind and a desire for spiritual renewal through religious faith. Rouault embraced Catholicism in 1895, and for some years his life and work were influenced by his friendship with the novelist Leon Bloy, a writer of spiritual but bitterly ironic tendencies. Rouault's subjects, often painted in series, were both religious and temporal: biblical subjects, acrobats, clowns, judges and landscapes. His sympathies were for the poor and down-trodden, and he commented that his imagination was stimulated by "the contrast between brilliant, scintillating things intended to amuse and this infinitely sad life." Rouault began his work as an engraver in 1917, illustrating many books and reaching his greatest heights in *Miserere et Guerre,* upon which he worked from 1927 until 1947. In 1947 Rouault regained a great many of his earlier paintings from the heirs of his dealer, Vollard. He destroyed some 315 of them that he considered imperfect and devoted the last ten years of his life to working on others in an effort to achieve the standard of perfection he had set for himself. Rouault remained constantly aloof from the great art movements of his time—Fauvism, Cubism and Surrealism—and painted consistently jewel-like works organized by line, endowed with a rich surface texture, and ceramic or glasslike in effect.

A Clown (1948)
This clown is a powerful expression of Rouault's compassion for the pain of humanity. The careworn face, ironically set off by the clown's costume, is grim and set in its expression; the landscape behind the clown is anguished and barren. Rouault's unique use of the stained-glass technique of bold color areas set off by heavy black lines suits the intense emotions he conveys in his portraits; the compassion that the artist felt for this clown awakens the same feelings in the viewer.

MAURICE UTRILLO

Maurice Utrillo (1883-1955) was born in Paris, the illegitimate child of Suzanne Valadon and an amateur painter and chronic alcoholic named Boissy. He was given the name Utrillo when he was eight years old by a Spanish art critic of that name. Maurice was an unhappy and neurotic child and his teen-age years were marked by increasing alcoholism. At the age of eighteen he had to be confined to an asylum. It was while he was shut away, the first of many such incarcerations for acute alcoholism, that he took up painting as a form of occupational therapy, encouraged by his mother. It soon became as necessary for him to paint as to drink, spending his nights in the cafes and his days behind an easel. During his periods of treatment in sanitoriums, he would paint from postcards. His scenes are those of the streets of Montmartre, where he associated loosely with the artists of the School of Paris who frequented the cafes, and of the Parisian suburbs, the quiet peaceful streets that surrounded the sanitoriums where he spent much of his time. His association with the artistic and intellectual circles dominant in Paris at the time was cursory; his mother, at one time the model and student of some of the giants of Impressionist painting was his primary teacher, as were the works of Sisley and Pissarro. Utrillo's adaptations of Impressionist landscapes are refreshing, simple and filled with a wry but loving commentary. Utrillo's paintings became enormously popular during his lifetime; by 1920 he had achieved a worldwide reputation and by 1920 he had received the Legion of Honor. But it was not until he was in his late fifties when he married a widow who watched over him carefully, that he gave up drinking entirely. He died a respectable citizen in a house the couple had purchased in a Paris suburb. Utrillo was an original artist, endowed with a talent for solid composition, a sure sense of color and an eye for simplifying and eliminating unnecessary details. Although his later paintings tended to be postcard-like repetitions of earlier canvases, his work at the height of his career exemplified a truly French sense of the endearing qualities of street and country landscapes.

A Street in the Suburbs (1916)
Painted in a light, almost Impressionistic manner, this street scene glints with sunlight and sparkles with a clean-washed feeling that suggests that a rain has recently fallen. Utrillo juxtaposes blues, greens and yellows to create a peaceful mood. The alley of trees, the long low white walls that pick up color from their surroundings and the long straight road all lead to a distant forest of trees that invites the eye. The steep traditional perspective, the delicate line and the harmonious color patterns are trademarks of Utrillo's works.

MAURICE DE VLAMINCK

Maurice de Vlaminck (1876-1958) was born in the heart of Paris, near Les Halles. His parents were both musicians of talent, although neither of them is well-known. Vlaminck began to draw while in elementary school and neglected his studies for his sketches. However, as he grew up he showed talent as a violinist and as a champion bicycle rider, so that he did not decide to become a painter until 1900, when he met Derain, a member of the group of artists who were to be known as the Fauves. The sight of Van Gogh's paintings further stimulated Vlaminck and he began to paint, without any academic studies. Vlaminck was a giant of a man with tremendous energy and as a young man he painted furiously in a brilliant orange, red and blue palette, writing novels and articles between paintings. The work of Van Gogh so stimulated him that bold colors and strong energetic brushstrokes were to remain staples of Vlaminck's canvases throughout his lifetime. In 1909, Vlaminck experimented briefly with Cubist constructions in his landscapes and still lifes and showed a preference in his palette for the pure whites and deep blues that are often to be found in his later works. After 1915, Vlaminck's palette became cooler and at the same time more dramatic in intensity, as he began to paint strong, stormy landscapes, overcast skies and lonely villages in a more solid but still turbulent style. He remained resolutely apart from all trends of contemporary art after his brief adventure into Cubism, and found in his return to nature a realistic outlet for his early Fauvist passion, remaining, however, true to the original influence of Van Gogh that colored all his works. In 1935, he retired to a large farm, La Rouilliere, near Beauce. Here he occupied himself with agriculture and continued to paint deeply-felt still lifes and sensitive landscapes that show an almost religious love of the land.

The Thatched Cottages
The countryside in this landscape is that of Vlaminck's family home and typically stretches out for miles. Thatched cottages such as this are a familiar form of architecture in this area, with roof overhanging whitewashed walls. Vlaminck's coloration was among the most intense of the Fauves and this canvas is a good illustration of his bold color and strong determined brushstroke. The strong thrust of movement along the vertical and the diagonal and the stormy thunderous sky are found repeatedly in his mature canvases. Paint is applied in thick slashing strokes to provide a rich, unctuous surface. The painting has an electric quality, as if it were illuminated by a flash of lightning that brings out the intensity of the colors.